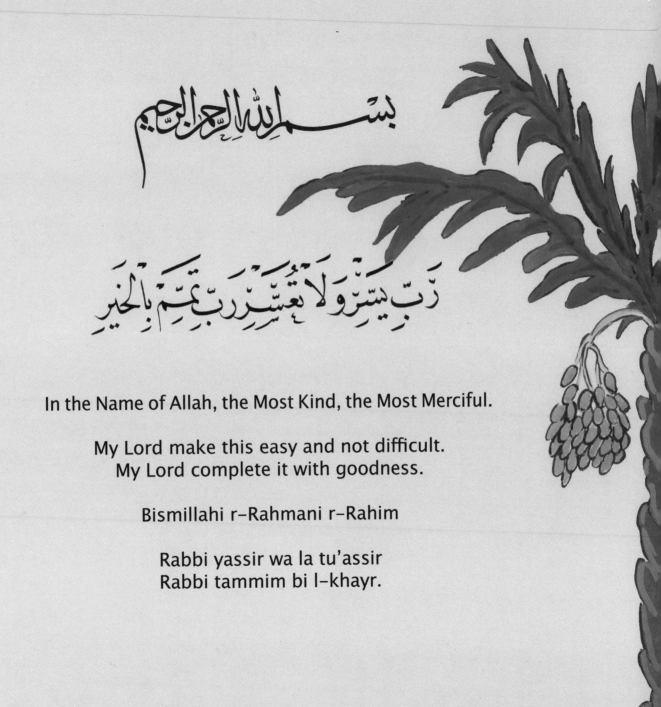

بِسْمِ اللَّهِ الرَّحْمَنِ الرَّحِيمِ

رَبِّ يَسِّرْ وَلَا تُعَسِّرْ رَبِّ تَمِّمْ بِالْخَيْرِ

In the Name of Allah, the Most Kind, the Most Merciful.

My Lord make this easy and not difficult.
My Lord complete it with goodness.

Bismillahi r–Rahmani r–Rahim

Rabbi yassir wa la tu'assir
Rabbi tammim bi l–khayr.

1

Printed in the United States of America

ISBN 978-0-9913003-1-0

Little Bird Books
littlebirdbooksink@gmail.com

Who Are You?

A Book of Very Serious Questions

By
Karima Sperling

Illustrated By
Alia Nazeer

This book is inspired by the teachings of Mawlana Sheikh Nazim Al-Haqqani. There is no way to thank him adequately for all he has given and all he has taught. So I ask Allah to please thank him for me and to give Mawlana all that he asks for and to open our hearts and minds to the important truths to which he tirelessly pointed the way.

"They do not rise above others only by means of their fasting and prayer but rather by their truthfulness, and the nobility of their intentions, having sound and wholesome hearts, giving sincere counsel by which they only desire the pleasure of Allah, with endless patience, totally merciful, humble without being meek. They do not see themselves as higher than anyone or envy those above them. They do not love the world, nor do they love for its sake."
(Hadith. Tirmidhi)

Dedication

To Ishaq who is full of questions. His father was reading The Quran one day and Ishaq began to jump on his lap. His father said, "Be careful this is Allah's Book." Ishaq said, "This is Allah's Book? How did *you* get it?"

MashaAllah, sometimes children see clearly the miracles we take for granted and sometimes the simplest questions are the most profound.

To my grandchildren of many questions: Haniya, Humayra, Hamza, Layka, Ibrahim, Ishaq and Ghalib; to Khalil and Noura who arrived in the middle; and to all the grandchildren of Adam (as) everywhere.

Thanks

Thanks to Allah our Most Generous Lord, who gave us eyes to see, ears to hear, a mind to understand at least some of it, and a heart to be most humbly grateful.

Thanks always to Aminah Sperling Alptekin for transforming our paper and computer files into a book, with her usual skill and artistic eye.

Thanks to Alia Sperling Nazeer, not only for her amazing paintings, but also for finishing them in the month before and after giving birth to a new little grandson of Adam (as).

Thanks to Dr. Munir Sperling for reading, for liking, for so many tasks undertaken cheerfully, small and large.

Thanks to Hajja Rukiye Sultan for liking the first draft and the safe, soft darkness; to Sanaa Makhlouf, Steffen AJ Stelzer and Yasmine Motawy – for their invaluable advice and encouragement.

Thanks to Xhengis Aliu of XL Studio and Bart Troyer of Allegra Printing for appearing out of the blue and rescuing us with their kindness and generosity.

1. OPENING

Find a nice place to sit and make yourself comfortable.
Open your eyes wide and shake yourself awake.
Get ready because
I have some very serious questions for you, my dearest.

Let us begin by saying,
Bismillahi r–Rahmani r–Rahim.
In the Name of Allah the Most Kind, the Most Merciful.

The Name of Allah is the key that opens locked doors; it is the sword that opens a way through difficulties.

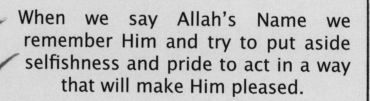

When we say Allah's Name we remember Him and try to put aside selfishness and pride to act in a way that will make Him pleased.

So let us say it
together and

open,
open,
open

and then walk
hand-in-hand through
the opening.

2. DO YOU KNOW WHO MADE YOU?

Allah made you.
Allah is One. He always was and He will always be.
La ilaha illa Allah

Allah is the Name of the One who made everything.
But He has many other names.
He is the Greatest, the Highest and the Mightiest.
He is the Most Beautiful and the Most Kind.
He is the Maker and the Caretaker.

All the Names of everything good belong to Him
and there is one of them that He gave to you, for
each one of us was made in the image of a different
one of His beautiful Names.
He also gave you His Name by calling you
His servant, Abd–Allah (for a boy) or
Amat–Allah (for a girl).

13

Will Allah ever die?

No He will not.

Will He ever disappear?

No He will not.

Does He ever sleep?

No He does not.

Does He ever get hungry?

No He does not.

Does He ever get thirsty?

No He does not.

Does He ever get tired?

No He does not.

Does He ever need anything?

No He does not.

Is He higher than the sky?

Yes He is.

Is He wider than the earth?

Yes He is.

Is He stronger than the mountain?

Yes He is.

Is He mightier than the sea?

Yes He is.

Is He gentler than your mother's kiss?

Yes He is.

Is He all that?

Yes He is – and more.

He is everything Good.

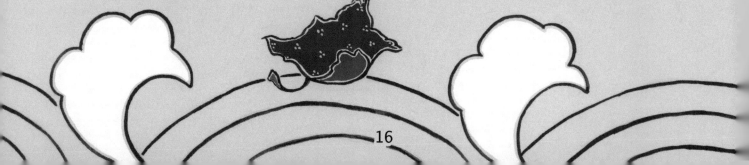

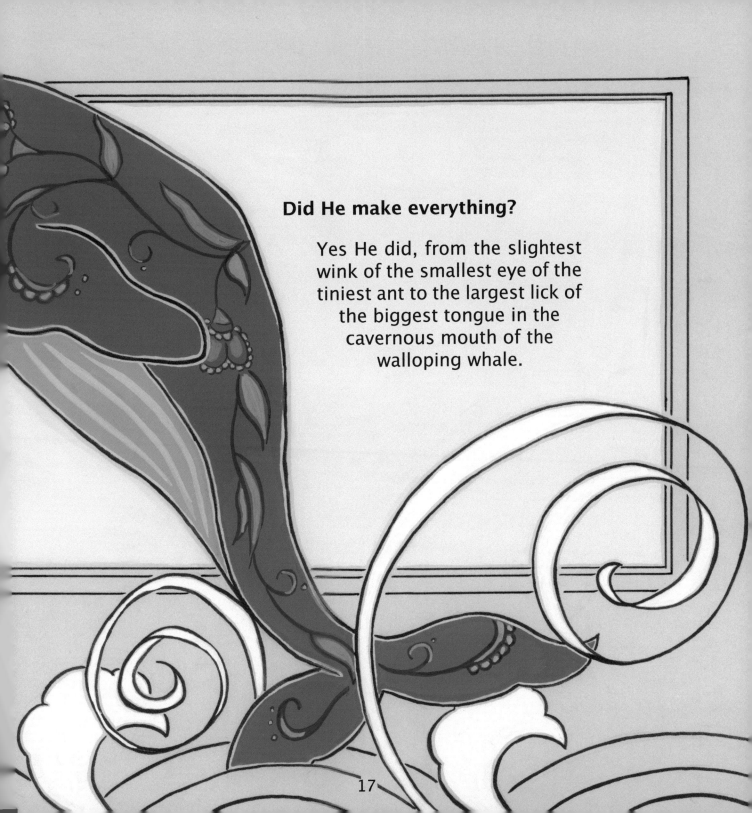

Did He make everything?

Yes He did, from the slightest wink of the smallest eye of the tiniest ant to the largest lick of the biggest tongue in the cavernous mouth of the walloping whale.

17

Does He see and know them all?

Yes He does.
Everything, even if it is buried at the bottom of the
deepest hole in the darkest earth or,
Is perched in the highest branches of the tallest tree
in the thickest forest or,
Is blanketed by mounds of the whitest snow on the
misty top of the mightiest mountain;
Even if it is swimming in the silent depths of a sunless
sea or,
Is floating high above the clouds in a night sky that
seems to go on forever –

Allah sees them all and knows each one by its
name.

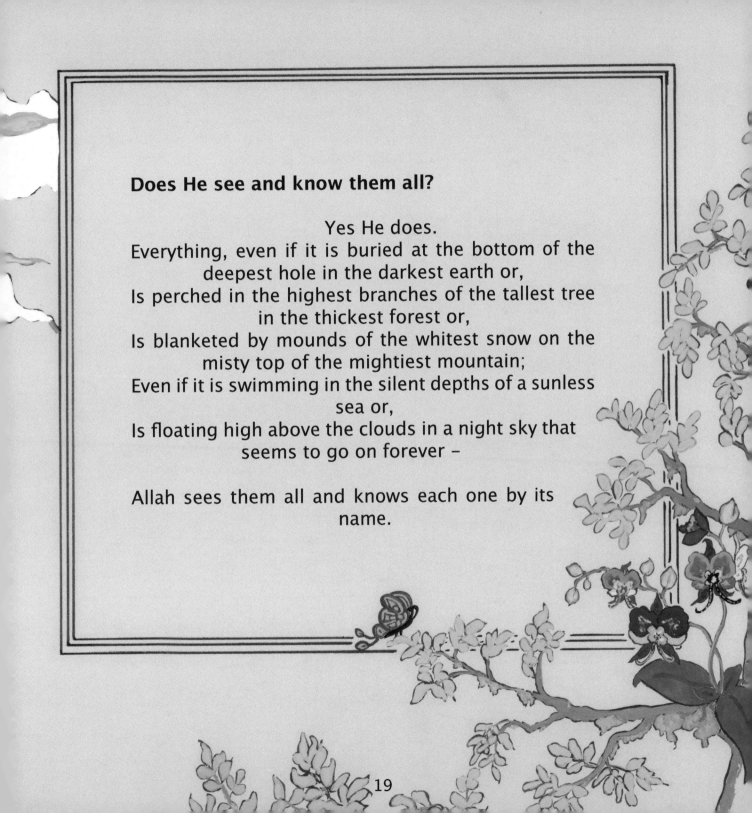

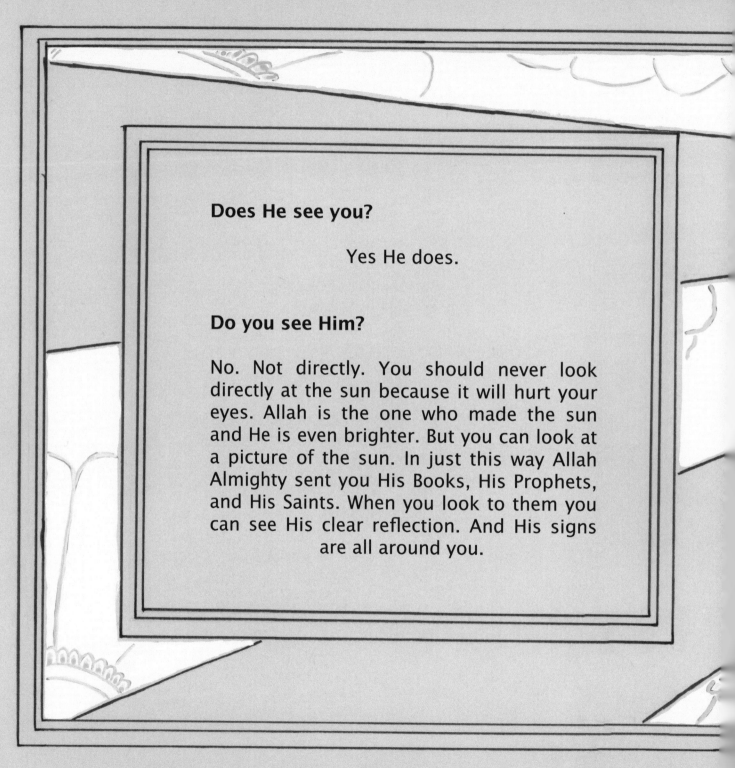

Does He see you?

Yes He does.

Do you see Him?

No. Not directly. You should never look directly at the sun because it will hurt your eyes. Allah is the one who made the sun and He is even brighter. But you can look at a picture of the sun. In just this way Allah Almighty sent you His Books, His Prophets, and His Saints. When you look to them you can see His clear reflection. And His signs are all around you.

Some of His signs are:

The night made for resting
And the day for learning.
The sun and rain for growing
The sweet fruits for tasting.
The stars for endless counting
And the clouds for dreaming.
The birds on spread wings gliding;
The spider at her spinning.
Family made for loving
And good friends for playing.
All of them clearly pointing
To the One who made them all.

However, you must believe in Him even if you
do not see Him and know that if you cannot
see Him, He, for sure, sees you.

Does He know your name?

Yes He does.

Does He know all about you, what you like and what you fear?

Yes He does.

Will He always hear you when you call to Him?

Yes He will. And He wants you always to call on Him, to ask from Him when you are in need.

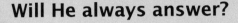

Will He always answer?

Yes He will, because He is the Answerer of Prayers. But you have to learn to understand His voice.

Will He always give you what is best?

Yes He will. But He will also give it at the time that He thinks best and you must know that what you want is not always what is best.

Will He always be there for you?

Yes always.

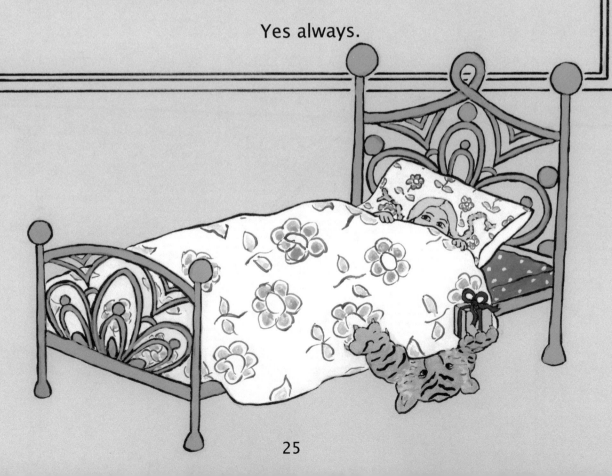

3. WHEN DID ALLAH MAKE YOU?

Allah made you a very, very, very long time ago.

Before there was this world as we know it, there was a smoky darkness; a rich, full, beautiful darkness that held within it – everything. All the light, all the power, all the beauty rested inside that soft, safe darkness.

Then Allah took some
of the light from out
of the darkness, His
light. From His light
He made another, the
light of the Prophet
Muhammad (sas).
From that light Allah
made many, many,
smaller lights, too many
for us to count. These are
the souls of everyone who
has ever lived or will ever
live from the very beginning
until the very end.

Was your soul among the little lights?
Yes. It was. Your soul and mine too and I knew
you and loved you even then.

Can you see your soul?
Yes you can. It is the shine in your loving eyes.

Can you touch your soul?
Yes you can. When you make someone happy you
have touched it.

Can you hear your soul?
Yes you can. When you say "Thank You" that is
its voice.

And these souls of light rested in the
peaceful, beautiful darkness for a very,
very long time.

Then what did Allah make?

Then Allah Almighty decided to make the world so He could see it and it could reflect Him. He made it all in six of His own special days, which are much longer than ours.

On Sunday the first day He made the Tablet and the Pen so they can record everything from the beginning until the end.
Then He made His Throne and His Court and the seven Heavens with Angels of light in every shape and sort.
Then of the hottest flames He made the seven layers of Hell and He made the communities of Jinn from fire as well.
Then He made the seven Earths with the sun to light the day and the moon to light the night and He hung the stars like lamps to shine.
Then He set them all in motion, counting off the hours and days, the months and

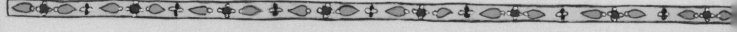

years, in the dance we call, Time.

Then He separated the dry land from the sea and made the mountains like pillars, the valleys like roads, and the vast plains like carpets with rivers flowing in the folds.

Then He made the eight Paradises, gardens through which jeweled rivers run, home for the good souls when their work on earth is done.

Then He made all the plants and living things, from the stubby mushroom to the towering tree; from the sticky spider to the stinging bee; from the proud lion to the timid deer; from the elegant horse to the lumbering bear.

Then when did He make you?

In the last minutes of Friday, Juma, when the world was only six days new, Allah Almighty made the final and most special creation of all: He made you.

4. HOW DID ALLAH MAKE YOU?

Allah made each thing in this world with one word. He said: "Kun" – "Be" and each one came into being.

Be! And it is. Kun fayakun.

Did He make you like that?

Yes but He also made you a little differently.

How then did Allah make you?

Allah Almighty ordered His trustworthy Angel to fly to earth and bring back a handful of dirt from every corner. The Angel returned carrying a handful of red dirt and one of black dirt and one of white dirt and one of brown dirt. These he gave to his Creator, Allah.

Allah mixed the earthly dirt with some water from Paradise and made clay. With His own hands Allah molded this clay into the most beautiful form. Then He breathed into him some of His own breath and added the little light that had been waiting.

Allah named this very first man – Adam (as) and he is your great, great, great grandfather and the great, great, great grandfather of every single person on this whole planet. Which means that we are all one family, brothers and sisters.

Allah made him perfect, beautiful, and strong, with eyes that see, and a mind that thinks, and a heart that understands. And the first thing that he did with his first breath was to thank his Creator.

So when you pass by a mirror and see your reflection, remember to thank Allah for making you so perfect, beautiful, and strong, with eyes that see, and a mind that thinks, and a heart that understands.

Then Allah dressed him with the cape of majesty and crowned him with the crown of light and put in his hand the sword of intention – Bismillahi r-Rahmani r-Rahim.

Then Allah ordered all the Angels in Heaven and all the newborn creatures on Earth to bow down and make sajda in front of Adam (as) because of the light of Muhammad (sas) that he carried.

What is the Sword of Bismillah?

It is Allah's sword that, if you are able to take it in your hand, will bring you happiness and success. It means that you make it your intention to put your hand in the Hand of Allah; that you lay aside what you want and do only what He wants in the way He wants it done. It means you will act out of love, never out of anger or fear. And it means you will pass by the things that do not concern you, with dignity.

Who is the Prophet Muhammad (sas)?

He is the most perfect, most beautiful, most loving person that Allah ever created. His light and his soul were the first to be made but he was born on earth as the last prophet. And Allah loves him so much that He calls him His Beloved.

Muhammad –
Allah's Beloved.
The Praised,
The one raised high.
When he spoke
The hard stones woke
In order to greet him.
Above his head a little cloud
Shaded him from a blazing sky.
The desert lion, wild and proud,
Traveled for miles in order to meet him.
The hungry wolf guarded the sheep
And didn't eat them.
The gazelle, usually so shy,
Came to lie by his side
And the lizard testified
To his being the Messenger of God.
For him the stiff trees bowed
And the palm tree sighed aloud
And a small plate of dates multiplied
To feed the crowd.
He is the one for whom the sun
Hung above the horizon
And for whom the moon split in half.
He is our guide on the path,
The perfect one,
The pride of creation,
Our Beloved –
Muhammad.

Allah so honored him that his name, Muhammad (sas), is right next to Allah's own Name, always and forever.

La ilaha illa Allah Muhammad Rasul Allah,

And whenever we say his name we ask Allah to pray on him and give him peace. Sallallahu alayhi wa sallam (sas). It pleases Allah when we love the one He loves.

Why was he sent?

It was through him that Allah gave us the Noble Quran, the book that contains knowledge about everything big or small and is a measure of all things good or bad. He was sent as a mercy to teach us and to show us the way to goodness. He is the perfect example of what it means to be a servant of Allah. When we follow him, we are rightly guided.

Is he like you?

Yes and no. He was a human being just like you. He ate, he slept, he laughed and he cried, just like you. But he loved Allah so much that nothing in all the world could make him forget or look away. So when he ate he remembered Allah and even when he slept he remembered Allah. When he laughed, he laughed for Allah and when he cried, he cried for Allah. And he carried the Bismillah in his hand and on his every breath.

Can you be like him?

If Allah is like the sun then the Prophet (sas) is like the moon, which reflects the sun's light in the darkness of the night. If you try you can be like a mirror so bright that it sparkles and shines with the soft moonlight.

How do you do that?

You can do that by trying to love the Prophet Muhammad (sas) so much that you want to follow in his footsteps in all things big or small.

Without the Prophet Muhammad (sas) we would never be able to answer all of these very serious questions.

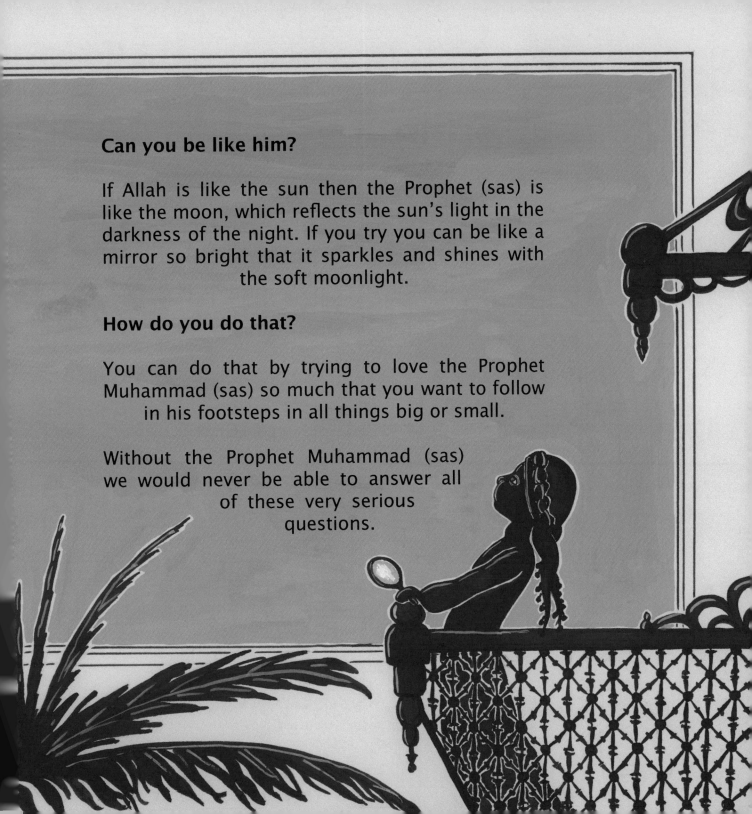

5. WHERE DID ALLAH MAKE YOU?

He made you in Paradise.

Where is Paradise?

Above the seven layers of Earth there are seven Heavens and these are home to myriads of Angels and heavenly beings that Allah created out of light. In the seventh and highest Heaven there are eight gates that lead to the eight levels of Paradise. The Paradises are flowering gardens with cool, clear, streams running through them.

Who lives there?

After the Judgment Day the souls of human beings, who have died on earth, continue to live in the beautiful palaces of Paradise with everything they could ever dream of wanting. They live there in peace and happiness in the company of the ones they love, for eternity. This is where you were made and where one day you will return, inshaAllah.

InshaAllah means, if God Wills. We must say this because if Allah wants, it will happen, and if He doesn't want then it will not happen. So when we say anything about what has not happened yet, we must always say, inshaAllah.

Is Allah in Paradise?

Yes. He is everywhere.

On Saturday, the seventh day, after all of the world had been made, and the planets set to spinning, and the sun and the moon to rising and setting, and the day and the night to taking their turns, and the hungry animals to searching for their food, and the people to building their houses and planting their fields; after all this, Allah Almighty raised Himself in His tremendous Majesty over His Mighty Throne.

What is His Throne?

The Glorious Throne of Allah, the symbol of His Power and Majesty, sits beyond a great ocean whose waves lap the shore of the eight Paradises, whose gates open into the seven Heavens, whose domes arch over the seven Earths, whose layers span the seven Hells. And they all swim in the oceans of their Lord's Mercy.
And, sea-to-sea, He rules them all with Love.

Is there a place where He is not?

No. There is no place where He is not. But in some places He seems closer than in others. The people in the lowest Paradise spend every joyful Juma in His Presence. The ones in the highest Paradise are always in His Presence. And Hell is what we call the place farthest away from Him.

Is He close to you?

Yes. He is as close to you as your beating heart.

Are you close to Him?

That depends on you. If you remember Him, He remembers you. You have to remember to feel close to Him.

Can you get closer?

Yes you can. Everything you do to please Him, to obey Him, brings you closer. And He says that for every step you take to get close to Him, He takes ten steps to get closer to you. If you come to Him walking, He comes to you running. He must love you very much.

So can you find Him?

Of course you can. There is nowhere else to go. He is where you came from and when you get there again you will say, "Oh, I am finally home."

Because you came from Allah and to Him you will return.

6. WHY DID ALLAH MAKE YOU?

He made you to know Him, to remember Him, to love and to serve Him.

He made you to be His Khalifa, to represent Him on earth. He made you out of the clay of the earth, the water of Heaven, and light from Himself. He taught you the names of everything so that, like Him, you can take care of them. And He set you above them all, Angel and animal, and told them to bow down to you because of the light of Muhammad (sas) that you carry and the respect and the honor Allah gave you.

Does this mean you are the king?

No. Allah is the King, the Sultan. There is, and can only be, One Sultan. We are His first and most honored servants.

Does this mean you can do whatever you want?

No. You must always do what it is that He would want you to do.

What does He want you to do?

He wants you to love Him and remember Him. He wants you to serve Him and treat all the things He made with love, giving to each one what it needs and what is its right.

How do you do that?

By doing your prayers and saying His Name; By loving and obeying your parents and being good to your family and neighbors; By being fair and kind to all you meet; By always saying the truth and never taking what isn't yours; By wishing for everyone the same goodness that you wish for yourself.

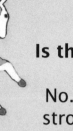

Is that all?

No. Sometimes you will have to be strong. Sometimes there is evil in the world.

When Allah ordered all of creation to bow before Adam (as) and the light of Muhammad (sas), all of them obeyed except one. That ugly, disobedient one, is shaytan, the devil. Out of jealousy for what Allah gave you and didn't give him, he has vowed to be your enemy. He wants you to forget Allah and serve him instead. You must always watch out for his tricks and his traps.

How do you stay safe?

If you remember Allah, shaytan cannot touch you.
If you say Allah's Name, shaytan cannot reach you.
If you run to Allah, shaytan cannot catch you.
So always remember, and say, and run.

And know that Allah is good, and the world He created is good, and He made it to serve you because you also are good. So you must be strong and keep yourself on the path that is right and try to set an example by your words and your deeds.

Hold tight to the heavenly sword of Bismillahi r–Rahmani r–Rahim; throw the cape of Majesty over your shoulder; wind the turban of honor around your crown of light and remain firm in the Name of Allah and – Do not be afraid!

Remember that good always triumphs over evil. If shaytan can turn a good thing bad, so Allah can turn a bad thing good. It is impossible that the bad will ever win or destroy the good. That is just how the world was made.

Never lose hope and don't worry.

Can you do all that?

Yes you can because Allah made you especially to do that. You were created for that purpose. He would never give you more than you can do. So be patient and call on Him, remember Him, and when the time is right He will strengthen your heart with Angels on flying horses, their turbans streaming behind them.

7. WHAT DID ALLAH MAKE YOU?

Did Allah make you a horse to run in circles on a track?
No He did not.
Did He make you a donkey to carry burdens on your back?
No He did not.
Did Allah make you a moose to butt your head and fight?
No He did not.
Did He make you a lion to roar and claw and bite?
No He did not.
Did He make you a parrot to screech and flap around?
No He did not.
Did He make you a rabbit afraid to make a sound?
No He did not.
Did He make you a pig to wallow in the mud?
No He did not.
Did He make you a mosquito to sting and suck the blood?
No He did not.
Did He make you a bear all grumbly in your den?
No He did not.

Did He make you a flighty, flightless hen?
No He did not.
Did He make you a sloth to hang limp in a tree?
No He did not.
Did He make you to clown around like a chimpanzee?
No He did not.
Did He make you to thump your chest like a gorilla?
No He did not.
Or show your bottom to the world like a mandrill–a?
No He certainly did not.

Allah made you to be good
And to fulfill His servanthood;
To be beautiful and kind;
To use your heart and use your mind
To protect those in your care
Like the earth, the sea, and air;
To guard the elephant and the ant
And not to be a tyrant.
To defend the tiger and the toucan –
That is why He made you Human.

8. SO THEN WHO ARE YOU?

You are one of the children of Adam (as).
You are Beautiful.
You are Prince and Princess of a remarkable world,
Honored and Honorable.
You are warriors for Truth –
Strong and Kind.
You are Light and you are Love.

You are obedient servants of the Sultan Most High:
Abdullah and Amatullah.
You carry His Light and His Trust.
You have His Help and His Support.
You are Clean and Good.

Now your job is to –

Remember.

Remember.

Remember.

And always try to keep yourself in the same perfect way
you were made and to protect the light that you were given.

And if you forget?

Then ask Allah to forgive you. And He will. He is the most Forgiving, the most Merciful, the most Kind. He understands.

And every night when you lie down in bed
and pull the covers up over your head,
say 3 times:

Allah is with me.
Allah looks after me.
Allah sees me.

And be at Peace.

9. DOES THAT ANSWER ALL OF YOUR QUESTIONS?

No. I am sure it does not. I am sure you can think of many, many more because one answer always gives rise to another question.

However, there are some questions whose answers we do not know and there are some answers that we do not understand. But one day, Allah has promised, He Himself will answer all of our questions. So we must be patient, for Allah does all things according to His own time.

And Allah knows all things best.

Notes

Pages 10-11

The use of the image of the sword is controversial in our times. It is an image that used to bring pride to the Muslims and now appears to bring shame. It is like the concept of Jihad/struggle: there is a greater jihad and a lesser jihad. The struggle against the ego, the internal enemy, is greater than that against an external enemy.

I tried to make the sword understandable to children as a symbol of the weapon in the struggle against the ego and the whisperings of shaytan. Only rarely, and under very specific circumstances, can a physical sword be used in jihad against anything else.

I didn't want to leave it out completely. Allah did not bring us into this world unarmed. We have a weapon to defend ourselves against our real enemies and that weapon is the remembrance of Allah. (Sheikh Nazim Al-Haqqani, sohbat: Saltanat.org)

"Therefore remember Me, I will remember you. Give thanks to Me, and reject not Me." (2:152) Pickthall translation.

"Any action not begun in the Name of Allah is incomplete (cut off)." Hadith (Al-Nasa'i)

Pages 12-13

Some of the Names of Allah
Al-Ahad - The One
Al-Kabir - The Great
Al-Ala - The High
Al-Aziz - The Mighty
Al-Jamal - The Beautiful. "Allah is beautiful and He loves beauty." Hadith (Sahih Muslim)
Al-Rahim- The Most Kind
Al-Khaliq - The Maker
Al-Wakil - The Caretaker

In the Picture: Al-Kabir on the mountain. Al-Khaliq on the tree. Al-Hafidh (the Preserver) on the white flower. Al-Jamal on the purple iris. Al-Rahim on the butterfly. Al-Ala on the cloud. Al-Jalil (The Majestic) - on the wave.

Pages 14-15

Ayatul Kursi (2:255)
"Allah! There is no God save Him, the Alive, the Eternal. Neither slumber nor sleep overtakes Him. Unto Him belong whatsoever is in the heavens and whatsoever is in the earth. Who is he who can intercede with

Him save by His leave? He knows that which is in front of them and that which is behind them while they encompass nothing of His knowledge save what He will. His throne includes the heavens and earth, and He is never weary of preserving them. He is the Sublime, the Tremendous." Quran Pickthall translation.

Pages 16-17

Abu Umama (ra) reported that the Messenger of Allah (sas) said: Allah and His Angels and the people of the heavens and the earth, even the ants in their rocks and the fish, pray for blessings on the Teacher of Goodness." Hadith (Tirmidhi)

"He knows what is in the land and the sea. Not a leaf falls but He knows it, not a grain amid the darkness of the earth, naught of wet or dry but it is in a clear record." (6:59) Quran Pickthall translation.

Pages 18-19

"Though it be the weight of a grain of mustard-seed, and though it be in a rock, or in the heavens, or in the earth, Allah will bring it forth." (31:16) Quran Pickthall translation.

The picture shows some creatures of legend (the Roc and her nest, the sea serpent) as well as natural treasures that are rare and hidden (jewels underground, rare orchids and insects found only on the tops of trees in the rain forests of the world).

Pages 20-21

"The Abdal (saints) in this community are 30. Their hearts are like the heart of Sayyiduna Ibrahim (as) the intimate of the All-Merciful (Khalilu r-Rahman). Whenever one of them dies Allah substitutes another in his place." Hadith (Imam Ahmad ibn Hanbal).
"The Abdal in this community are 30. By them the earth is established, and by them you are sent rain, and by them you are granted help and victory." Hadith (Tabarani)

Pages 22-23

"A man dressed in spotless white came to see the Prophet (sas) when he was sitting among his Companions in Medina. Nobody knew him or recognized him but he sat down knee to knee with the Prophet (sas) and began asking questions.
First he asked: O Muhammad, what is Islam?
The Prophet replied: Islam is that you say La ilaha illa Allah Muhammadu r-Rasul Allah, pray, give charity, fast Ramadan, and make Hajj if you are able.
Then he asked: What is Iman?
The Prophet replied: It is to believe in Allah, His Angels, His Books, His Messengers, The Last Day, Destiny - its good and its bad.
Then he asked: What is Ihsan?

The Prophet replied: It is that you serve Allah as if you can see Him for although you may not see Him, know that He for sure sees you.

Then he asked: Tell me about the Hour and its signs.

The Prophet replied: The one questioned knows as little as the one asking the question. Its signs are that the slave gives birth to her mistress, and that the poor, naked shepherds compete with each other to build tall buildings.

To each answer the stranger remarked on its correctness and the Companions were amazed. After he left, Sayyidina Umar (ra) asked the Prophet (sas) who the man was. He told him that he was the Angel Jibrail (as) come to teach them their religion." Hadith (Sahih Muslim)

Pages 24–25

The animals, which represent things that might be frightening to children, are actually holding gifts because even within our fears and difficulties there are gifts from Allah.

"Verily from among My slaves is he whose faith cannot be rectified except by being afflicted with poverty, and were I to enrich him, it would surely corrupt him. Verily from among My slaves is he whose faith cannot be rectified except by wealth and affluence, and were I to deprive him, it would surely corrupt him. Verily from among My slaves is he whose faith cannot be rectified except by good health, and were I to make him sick, it would surely corrupt him. Verily from among My slaves is he whose faith cannot be rectified except by illness and disease, and were I to make him healthy, it would surely corrupt him. Verily from among My slaves is he who seeks worship by a certain act but I keep that from him so that self amazement does not enter his heart. Certainly I run the affairs of My slaves by My knowledge of what is in their hearts. Certainly I am the All-Knower, the All-Aware." Hadith Qudsi (Tabarani)

"And if My servant asks you about Me – behold, I am near; I respond to the call of him who calls, whenever he calls unto Me: let them then respond unto Me, and believe in Me, so they might follow the right way." (2:186) Quran Asad translation.

Al-Mujib: The Answerer of Prayers, one of Allah's 99 Names.

Pages 26–27

See At-Tabari, At-Tarikh vol.1. H. Amina Adil, Lore of Light vol.1. Ath-Thalabi, Qisas Al-Anbiya. The Stories of the Creation differ from one source to another. I chose a pretty general sequence of events not following any one particular telling but trying to be true to all of them.

The picture is the Arabic word 'bism' meaning, in the name of. It is said that the essence of the Quran is contained in the Fatihah, and the essence of the Fatihah is in the Bismillah, and the essence of the Bismillah is contained in its first letter, ba, and the essence of the ba is in the dot (nuqta) beneath it, which represents the essential Unity. An-Nasafi, Tafsir Madarik at-Tanzil.

"He it is who created the heavens and earth in six days and is moreover established on the Throne (of Authority). He knows what enters within the earth and what comes forth out of it, what comes down from heaven and what mounts up to it. And He is with you wheresoever you may be. And He sees well all that you may do." (57:4) Quran Yusuf Ali translation.

"Have not those who disbelieve known that the heavens and the earth were of one piece, then We parted them, and We made every living thing of water? Will they not believe?

And We have placed in the earth firm hills lest it quake with them, and We have placed therein ravines as roads that haply they may find their way.

And we have made the sky a roof withheld (from them) and yet they turn away from the signs. And He it is who appointed the night and the day, and the sun and the moon. They float each in an orbit." (21: 30–33) Quran Pickthall translation.

"To Him is due the primal origin of the heavens and earth: When He decrees a matter, He says to it: 'Be', and it is." (2:117) QuranYusuf Ali translation.

The picture is the Arabic word 'Kun' – 'Be'. It is said: "Nobody knows what lies between the letter kaf (K) and the letter nun (N)."

"(Allah) said, O Iblis! What prevents you from prostrating yourself to one I have created with My hands?" (38:75) Quran Yusuf Ali translation.

"Say: It is He who has created you and made for you the faculties of hearing, seeing, feeling, and understanding: little thanks do you give." (67:23) Quran Yusuf Ali translation.

I have called this the Sword of intention because intention, niyat, is a central concept in Islam. You will be judged by your intentions (Hadith Bukhari). So it is important to introduce to children the idea of considering, before they act, what is their purpose, their true intention.

"…When I love someone I am his hearing with which he hears, his seeing with which he sees, his hand with which he strikes and his foot with which he walks…" Hadith Qudsi (Bukhari)

"'When I have fashioned him and breathed into him of My spirit, fall down in obeisance unto him.' So the Angels prostrated themselves, all of them together." (15:29–30) Quran Yusuf Ali translation.

"And those who will not witness vanity, but when they pass near senseless play, pass by with dignity." (25:72) Quran Pickthall translation.

The Prophet (sas) is called HabibAllah – the Beloved of Allah.

The "one raised high" refers to the Isra and Mihraj – the Night Journey when Allah Almighty invited the Prophet (sas) to visit all of creation including the Earths, Heavens and Hells and then to approach to within two bow lengths of the indescribable Majesty of the Lord Himself.

Stones
Sayyida Aisha (ra) reported that the Prophet (sas) said: "When Jibrail (as) brought me the message, I would never pass by a rock or a tree without it saying, "Peace be upon you, O Messenger of God." Hadith (Qadi Iyad: Ash-Shifa).

Cloud
When the Prophet (sas) traveled to Syria with his uncle Abu Talib (ra), the monk Bahira, looking out from his retreat high on a hill, noticed a small cloud that seemed to be moving consistently over the head of one of the members of a traveling caravan. Bahira knew from his holy books that this was a sign of the coming Prophet and he invited all the men of that caravan to a meal. Not finding the one he was looking for among his guests he asked if they had left anyone behind. Abu Talib (ra) replied that the only one not present was his orphan nephew who was left to keep watch over the animals and the baggage. Bahira asked for him and saw that he was Muhammad, the Prophet he was waiting for. Hadith (At-Tabari)

Lion
The companion of the Prophet (sas) As-Safina (ra) was left in Yemen to teach Islam to the people. On his return journey he was accosted by a wild lion. When he called out "Leave me alone, I am a servant of the Messenger of Allah" the lion stopped growling and pulled back. The lion continued to accompany him all the way back to Medina and even showed him the way when he got lost. Hadith (Tabrizi: Al-Mishkat Al-Musabih)

Wolf
Ahban ibn Aus (ra) said that he was pasturing his sheep when a wolf grabbed one of them and tried to kill and eat it. Ahban (ra) rescued the sheep from the jaws of the hungry wolf and chased it away with his staff. The wolf turned and reproached Ahban (ra), asking him on what grounds did the shepherd deny the wolf his rightful provision. The shepherd drew back in surprise and exclaimed what a wonderful thing it was to hear a wolf speak. The wolf answered that if he wanted to witness something even more wonderful he should go over the hill to where the Prophet of God was living in Medina. The shepherd said that he would like to go but had no one with whom to leave his sheep. The wolf then offered to watch the sheep for the shepherd.
So Ahban (ra) left to visit the Prophet (sas) and become Muslim. When he returned he found the wolf and all his sheep safely where he had left them. He slaughtered one of the sheep and gave it as thanks to the wolf and continued to tell this miraculous story till the end of his days. Hadith (Bukhari).

Gazelle

The wife of the Prophet (sas) Umm Salama (ra) related the story of the mother gazelle who had been trapped by a hunter. The gazelle spoke to the Prophet (sas) and asked him to free her so that she could take her two babies to a safe place to hide them. The Prophet (sas) asked her to promise to return after she looked after her children because she was the property of the hunter and it was not the Prophet's (sas) right to let her go. After some time the gazelle returned and lay beside the Prophet (sas) allowing him to do with her as he wished. The Prophet (sas) asked the hunter to release her and he did. She thanked them both and bounded back into the hills to join her babies. Hadith (Al-Haythami: Majma al Zawa'id)

Lizard

Umar ibn ul-Khattab (ra) reported that a Bedouin came to the Prophet (sas) holding a lizard that he had caught for food. He said to the Prophet (sas) that he would believe in him when the lizard believed in him. At that the lizard testified that "Muhammad is the Messenger of Allah" so loudly that all those present witnessed the miracle. The Bedouin took the hand of the Prophet (sas) and accepted Islam. Hadith (Ibn Kathir: Al-Bidaya wa n-Nihaya)

Bowing Trees

Ibn Abbas (ra) reports that an Arab of the desert was invited by the Prophet (sas) to enter Islam. He replied rudely that he would believe if the date palm growing nearby believed first. By this he meant to say that he would never believe because he thought it was impossible for a tree to speak and be a believer. The Prophet (sas) called to the date palm and it moved closer to him and bowed. Then the tree spoke in a deep voice – La ilaha illa Allah Muhammadu r-Rasul Allah. The Prophet (sas) then signaled for the palm to return to its former place, which it did. The man accepted Islam without further argument. Hadith (Tirmidhi)

And Sayyidina Ali (ra) related that when he went around Mecca in the company of the Prophet (sas) the stones would give him salams and the trees would bow down before him. Hadith (Tirmidhi)

Palm Tree Sighed

In the beginning the Prophet (sas) used to lean on a palm tree trunk when he gave the sohbat after prayer in Medina. Then his companions built him a pulpit to lean on. The palm tree was heard to sigh and cry like a baby. The Prophet (sas) stopped his sohbat and went to put his arm around the tree to comfort it because it missed his touch and his nearness. Hadith narrated by Sayyidina Umar ibn ul-Khattab (ra). (Bukhari)

Dates

Amra bint Ruwaha (ra) related that when she was a little girl her mother gave her a small basket of dates to take to her father and uncle when they were digging the trench before the battle of Khandaq. On her way she met the Prophet (sas) who beckoned her over and asked to see what she had in her basket. She dumped the dates into the hands of the Prophet (sas) and they did not even fill his cupped hands. He had a cloth spread and he scattered the dates over the cloth then called all the Companions who were digging the trench to come eat. They came in small groups and each ate his fill and still there remained dates on the cloth as if none had been taken. The whole army ate from a handful of dates. Hadith (Ibn Ishaq)

Sun

On his return from Khaybar, the Prophet (sas) set up camp in the late afternoon. He lay his head in Sayyidina Ali's (ra) lap and revelation came upon him. Sayyidina Ali (ra) did not want to disturb the Prophet (sas) so he sat quietly until the sun set and the Prophet arose. He asked Sayyidina Ali (ra) if he had prayed Asr prayer to which he replied that he had not. The Prophet (sas) signaled to the sun to return to the sky and the two of them prayed Asr. Then it set and they prayed Maghrib. Hadith (Tahawi)

Moon

The Quraish demanded that the Prophet (sas) show them a miracle in order to believe in him. He pointed his finger at the moon and Allah split the moon in half. This was seen clearly by the unbelieving Quraish but they explained it away by calling it a magic trick. Hadith reported by Abdullah ibn Mas'ud (ra) (Sahih Muslim)

"The hour is nigh and the moon is cleft asunder. If they see a sign they turn away, and say, 'This is (but) transient magic.'" (54:1-2) Quran Yusuf Ali translation.

Pages 38–39

"Allah and His angels send blessings on the Prophet: O you that believe, send blessings on him and salute him with all respect." (33:56) Quran Yusuf Ali translation.

It was said that the Prophet (sas) had certain physical qualities that distinguished him from other men. His sight was far and clear. He hearing was exceptionally keen. He had a beautiful scent that emanated from his body so that the Companions could tell what path he had gone down just by the trace in the air of his perfumed sweat. But he also stayed aware during his sleep and continued to be conscious of what happened around him. It is recorded that he slept and rose to pray without making ablution (a requirement after sound sleep). Hadith (Sahih Muslim).

Sayyida Aisha (ra) was asked what the Prophet (sas) was like, by someone who had never met him. She answered that he was like the Quran walking. Hadith (Sahih Muslim).

Pages 40–41

"Verily in the Messenger of Allah you have a good example for who looks to Allah and the last day, and remembers Allah much." (33:21) Quran Pickthall translation.

Pages 44–45.

He it is who created the heavens and earth in six days – and His throne was over the waters – that He might try you, which of you is best in conduct. (11:7) Quran Pickthall translation.

"So they acknowledge their sins; but far removed are the dwellers in the flames." (67:11) Quran Pickthall translation.

Pages 46–47

"It was We who created man, and We know what dark suggestions his soul makes to him: for We are nearer to him than (his) jugular vein." (50:16) Quran Pickthall translation.

"Allah says, 'I am as My servant expects Me to be, and I am with him when he remembers Me. If he thinks of Me, I think of him. If he mentions Me in company, I mention him in even better company. When he comes closer to Me by a hand span, I come closer to him by an arm's length. If he draws closer to Me by an arm's length, I draw closer by a distance of two outstretched arms nearer to him. If My servant comes to Me walking, I go to him running." Hadith (Bukhari)

"Love of the homeland is part of faith." This is a disputed Hadith one of whose meanings, which is not disputed, is that to love and long for your true place of origin is part of faith.

"Who say, when afflicted by calamity: 'To Allah we belong and to Him is our return' –inna lillahi wa inna ilayhi raji'un." (2:156) Quran Yusuf Ali translation.

Pages 48–49

"I created the jinn and humankind only that they might worship Me." (51:56) Quran Pickthall translation.

Allah said: "I was a hidden treasure and I loved to be known, so I created the world so that I could be known." Hadith Qudsi.

"None of you (truly) believes until he wishes for his brother what he wishes for himself." Hadith (An-Nawawi's 40 Hadith #13)

Pages 50–51

"Do not look for a fight with the enemy. Beg God for peace and security. But if you do end up facing the enemy, then show endurance and remember that Paradise is under the shadow of swords." Hadith (Sahih Muslim)

"...On no soul does Allah place a burden greater than it can bear..." (2:286) Quran Pickthall translation.

"...Despair not of the Mercy of Allah for Allah forgives all sins..." (39:53) Quran Yusuf Ali translation.

"When you sought help of your Lord and He answered you: I will help you with a thousand of the Angels, rank on rank. Allah appointed it only as good tidings, and that your hearts might thereby be at rest.

Victory comes only by Allah. Lo! Allah is Mighty, Wise." (8:9–10) Quran Pickthall translation.

At the Battle of Badr some of the companions felt the presence of the angels, "Others had glimpses of the Angels riding on horses whose hooves never touched the ground, led by Gabriel wearing a yellow turban, whereas the turbans of the other angels were white, with one end left streaming behind them." (Lings: Muhammad, p. 148)

"O you who believe! Seek help with patient perseverance and prayer; for Allah is with those who patiently persevere." (2:153) Quran Yusuf Ali translation.

Pages 54–55

"O you who believe! Remember Allah with much remembrance." (33:41) Quran Pickthall translation.

Pages 56–57

"... for man was created weak." (4:28) Quran Pickthall translation. Even the weak and forgetful part of man was designed by the Creator. The purpose is to remember and turn again to Allah.

It is related by Imam Al-Ghazali that Sahl at-Tustari, a 9th century Sufi, said about himself: "When I was a boy of 3, I used to get up at night and watch my uncle, Muhammad bin Muhammad bin Suwar in his seclusion. So my uncle asked me one day, 'Why don't you remember God who created you?' I asked, 'How shall I remember Him?' Say in your heart when you get under your bedding, three times, without moving your tongue: God is with me, God is looking after me, God is beholding me. (Allah ma'i ,Allah shahidi, Allah nazari.) So I said it some few nights, then informed him. He told me to say it seven times every night. I did so and told him of it. He told me to do it every night eleven times. I did so, whence its sweetness sank into my heart." (p.259 Al-Ghazali: Mukhtasar ihya 'ulum ad-din. Spohr Publishers Limited, Nikosia Cyprus. Translator: H. Marwan Khalaf).

"But if they (your parents) strive to make you join in worship with Me things of which you have no knowledge, obey them not; yet bear them company in this life with justice (and consideration), and follow the way of those who turn towards Me (in love): in the end the return of you all is to Me, and I will tell you the truth (and meaning) of all that you did." (31:15) Quran Yusuf Ali translation.